WISDOM FOR KIDS

BOOK 2: Wisdom Has Rewards!

ADAPTED BY: T.L. Martínez   ILLUSTRATED BY: James Koenig

Wisdom For Kids - Book 2: Wisdom Has Rewards!

By Tito and Liz Martínez

Copyright © 2021 by Tito and Liz Martínez - www.lionstalesbooks.com

Illustrations by James Koenig - www.freelancefridge.com

Coloring by Marshal Uhls - www.marshaluhls.artstation.com

ISBN 978-1-7369409-5-2

tlmartinez@lionstalesbooks.com

Wisdom for Kids: Book 3 Coming Soon

For Enzo and Kate. May the Lord bless you and keep you. May he make his face shine upon you and be gracious to you. May he give you his favor and give you his peace.

- T.L. Martínez -

To my future children, we pray for you every day and look forward to seeing the amazing children of God you will become.

- James Koenig -

A Note To Parents:

As Christian parents, we are always seeking to bring God's word to life for our own children. Both of us grew up reading Proverbs as children in family devotions — each in our native languages. In writing this series, we sought to find a creative way to present the book of Proverbs to our kids, personifying the character traits described throughout Proverbs.

As a bilingual family, we referenced several versions of the Bible in both English and Spanish to help us write each book. Our goal in this series is to adapt each chapter of Proverbs, verse by verse, line by line — not leaving out anything but simply making it fun and understandable for even the youngest children.

And you must commit yourselves wholeheartedly to these commands that I am giving you today. Repeat them again and again to your children. Talk about them when you are at home and when you are on the road, when you are going to bed and when you are getting up. Tie them to your hands and wear them on your forehead as reminders. Write them on the doorposts of your house and on your gates. (Deut. 6:6-9)

Hi, Kids! Good to see you again. Guess what? I have some more advice for you. This advice is extra important, so treasure it and guard it with your life.

Tune in to the World of Wisdom. Try with all your heart to grasp Understanding. Finding Wisdom should be your priority. Even if you get lost on your quest, don't give up until you find her.

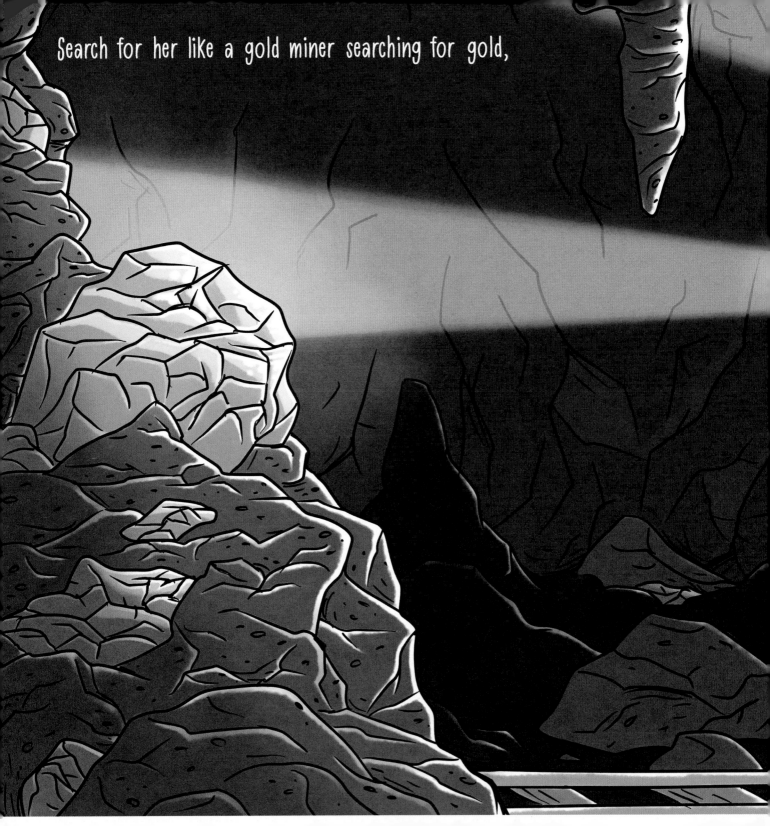

like an explorer on a treasure hunt.

Then, you will understand what it means to obey the LORD, and you will begin to know GOD.

Here's the best part: GOD gives you Wisdom when you ask him. Knowledge and Understanding can only come from him.

GOD gives you Wisdom and Good Sense when you tell the truth.

When you treat others kindly and fairly, he watches the road ahead for you.

Like a bodyguard, he protects you when you are loyal and faithful to him.

Now, see if you can find the best traits: honesty, fairness, loyalty and right living. Can you see them?

When you choose to follow my counsel, Captain Wisdom will be your friend,

and Knowledge the Liberator will be your ally.

Ranger Goodsense will scout ahead for danger.

And Understanding the Insightful Guardian will keep you safe.

These friends will keep you from making wrong turns on this journey of life. They'll make sure that you don't take bad directions from people who are so lost they can't even tell the difference between a trail and a troll.

These wise friends will keep you from following people who use bad words and do bad things. They'll make sure you don't leave Wisdom's Way to take a dark and scary path.

Your wise friends will help you stay away from people who betray even their closest friends. They don't keep their promises to GOD or other people, so don't even hang out at their houses.

People like this are walking towards certain death. If you follow them, you'll never make it back to the Way of Wisdom.

So, join the team of these good friends and follow them on this path of life. You can trust them - they really know where they're going.

Kids like you, who are honest and do the right thing (even when no one is watching), are the ones who will make it to their destination in life.

About The Authors:

Tito and Liz Martínez live in Houston, TX with their two children. Tito is a native of San Salvador, El Salvador while Liz is a transplanted Houstonian. The couple met in church in 2008 and married on top of the Quezaltepeque volcano (El Boquerón) in San Salvador in 2013. Liz owns her own children's services agency and holds a Master of Educational Psychology from the University of Houston, while Tito runs his own marketing company and studied Theology at Universidad Evangélica de El Salvador. As the founders of Lion's Tales, Wisdom for Kids is their first series of children's books.

Author email:

tlmartinez@lionstalesbooks.com

Website:

www.lionstalesbooks.com

About The Illustrator and Colorist:

James Koenig and Marshal Uhls have worked together on projects for many years. They originally teamed up on a large character development line with a tight deadline. They quickly discovered they enjoyed collaborating and have grown into a great team, creating spectacular books and designs together. James illustrates the pages and Marshal colors the drawings.

James has illustrated 50 children's books (and counting) and has created characters and illustrations for countless other children's toys and products over the last 15 years.

Marshal has illustrated for video games and other products for over 10 years. He has a knack for matching the illustration styles that James creates. The vibrancy he creates while coloring brings out the best in the books they work on together.

You can learn more about them at: www.freelancefridge.com.

References:

Biblia para todos: Traducción en lenguaje actual. (2003). Brasil: Sociedades Bíblicas Unidas.

Holy Bible: International Children's Bible. (1999). Nashville, TN: Tommy Nelson.

Holy Bible. New Living Translation. (2005). Wheaton, IL: Tyndale House.

La Biblia: Dios Habla Hoy. (2013). Sociedades Bíblicas Unidas.

La Palabra de Dios Para Todos: La Biblia de las Américas. (1975). México: The Lockman Foundation.

La Santa Biblia: Nueva Versión Internacional. (2004). Miami, FL: Sociedad Bíblica Internacional.

The Holy Bible: King James version. (2014). Peabody, MA: Hendrickson.

The Holy Bible, New International Version. (1984). Grand Rapids: Zondervan Publishing House.

The Message. (2004). Colorado Springs, CO: NavPress.

Santa Biblia: Antiguo y Nuevo Testamento. (2016). Nashville, TN: Holman Bible.

Santa Biblia: Nueva Traducción Viviente. (2018). Carol Stream, IL: Tyndale House.

Young's Literal Translation of the Holy Bible. (1977). Grand Rapids, MI: Baker Book House.

Collect all the books in the Wisdom for Kids series.

All books are available on:

 •  •

... and many other places you purchase books online!

BOOK 1: The Purpose of Proverbs
in English

LIBRO 1: El Propósito de los Proverbios
en Español

BOOK 2: Wisdom Has Rewards!
in English

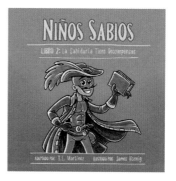

LIBRO 2: La Sabiduría Tiene Recompensas
en Español

Made in the USA
Coppell, TX
15 January 2022

71677112R00031